GREAT
AMERICAN PRESIDENTS

JOHN QUINCY
ADAMS

GREAT
AMERICAN PRESIDENTS

JOHN ADAMS

JOHN QUINCY ADAMS

JIMMY CARTER

THOMAS JEFFERSON

JOHN F. KENNEDY

ABRAHAM LINCOLN

RONALD REAGAN

FRANKLIN DELANO ROOSEVELT

THEODORE ROOSEVELT

HARRY S. TRUMAN

GEORGE WASHINGTON

WOODROW WILSON

——————— GREAT ———————
AMERICAN PRESIDENTS

JOHN QUINCY
ADAMS

MARTHA S. HEWSON

FOREWORD BY
WALTER CRONKITE

CHELSEA HOUSE
PUBLISHERS
A Haights Cross Communications Company

Philadelphia

DEDICATION
For Jackie Ziegler and Craig Ziegler, with many thanks
for sharing your books, and for Kay Winters, who told me
about the alligator in the White House.

CHELSEA HOUSE PUBLISHERS

VP, NEW PRODUCT DEVELOPMENT Sally Cheney
DIRECTOR OF PRODUCTION Kim Shinners
CREATIVE MANAGER Takeshi Takahashi
MANUFACTURING MANAGER Diann Grasse

STAFF FOR JOHN QUINCY ADAMS

ASSOCIATE EDITOR Kate Sullivan
PRODUCTION EDITOR Megan Emery
ASSISTANT PHOTO EDITOR Noelle Nardone
SERIES DESIGNER Keith Trego
COVER DESIGNER Keith Trego
LAYOUT 21st Century Publishing and Communications, Inc.

A Haights Cross Communications ✦ Company

www.chelseahouse.com

First Printing

1 3 5 7 9 8 6 4 2

Library of Congress Cataloging-in-Publication Data applied for.

ISBN 0-7910-7599-0

TABLE OF CONTENTS

FOREWORD

WALTER CRONKITE

A candle can defy the darkness. It need not have the power of a great searchlight to be a welcome break from the gloom of night. So it goes in the assessment of leadership. He who lights the candle may not have the skill or imagination to turn the light that flickers for a moment into a perpetual glow, but history will assign credit to the degree it is due.

Some of our great American presidents may have had a single moment that bridged the chasm between the ordinary and the exceptional. Others may have assured their lofty place in our history through the sum total of their accomplishments.

When asked who were our greatest presidents, we cannot fail to open our list with the Founding Fathers who put together this nation and nursed it through the difficult years of its infancy. George Washington, John Adams, Thomas Jefferson, and James Madison took the high principles of the revolution against British tyranny and turned the concept of democracy into a nation that became the beacon of hope to oppressed peoples around the globe.

Almost invariably we add to that list our wartime presidents—Abraham Lincoln, perhaps Woodrow Wilson, and certainly Franklin Delano Roosevelt.

Nonetheless there is a thread of irony that runs through the inclusion of the names of those wartime presidents: In many aspects their leadership was enhanced by the fact that, without objection from the people, they assumed extraordinary powers to pursue victory over the nation's enemies (or, in the case of Lincoln, the Southern states).

The complexities of the democratic procedures by which the United States Constitution deliberately tried to withhold unchecked power from the presidency encumbered the presidents who needed their hands freed of the entangling bureaucracy that is the federal government.

Much of our history is written far after the events themselves took place. History may be amended by a much later generation seeking a precedent to justify an action considered necessary at the latter time. The history, in a sense, becomes what later generations interpret it to be.

President Jefferson in 1803 negotiated the purchase of vast lands in the south and west of North America from the French. The deal became knows as the Louisiana Purchase. A century and a half later, to justify seizing the nation's steel mills that were being shut down by a labor strike, President Truman cited the Louisiana Purchase as a case when the president in a major matter ignored Congress and acted almost solely on his own authority.

The case went to the Supreme Court, which overturned Truman six to three. The chief justice, Fred Vinson, was one of the three justices who supported the president. Many historians, however, agreed with the court's majority, pointing out that Jefferson scarcely acted alone: Members of Congress were in the forefront of the agitation to consummate the Louisiana Purchase and Congress voted to fund it.

With more than two centuries of history and precedent now behind us, the Constitution is still found to be flexible when honest and sincere individuals support their own causes with quite different readings of it. These are the questions that end up for interpretation by the Supreme Court.

As late as the early years of the twenty-first century, perhaps the most fateful decision any president ever can make—to commit the nation to war—was again debated and precedent ignored. The Constitution says that only the Congress has the authority to declare war. Yet the Congress, with the objection of few members, ignored this Constitutional provision and voted to give President George W. Bush the right to take the United States to war whenever and under whatever conditions he decided.

Thus a president's place in history may well be determined by how much power he seizes or is granted in re-interpreting and circumventing the remarkable document that is the Constitution. Although the Founding Fathers thought they had spelled out the president's authority in their clear division of powers between the branches of the executive, the legislative and the judiciary, their wisdom has been challenged frequently by ensuing generations. The need and the demand for change is dictated by the march of events, the vast alterations in society, the global condition beyond our influence, and the progress of technology far beyond the imaginations of any of the generations which preceded them.

The extent to which the powers of the presidency will be enhanced and utilized by the chief executives to come in large degree will depend, as they have throughout our history, on the character of the presidents themselves. The limitations on those powers, in turn, will depend on the strength and will of those other two legs of the three-legged stool of American government—the legislative and the judiciary.

And as long as this nation remains a democracy, the final say will rest with an educated electorate in perpetual exercise of its constitutional rights to free speech and a free and alert press.

1

A STUDENT
OF THE WORLD

IN FEBRUARY 1778, John Adams was going to France to seek help for the American Revolution. Winter voyages across the stormy Atlantic Ocean were always risky, but this trip would be especially dangerous. If a British warship captured his ship, Adams would be taken prisoner and hanged for treason. He had signed the Declaration of Independence in 1776 and was well known in Great Britain as a leader of the revolution. Adams had managed to persuade his wife, Abigail, to stay at their farm in Braintree, Massachusetts, but one member of the family begged to come along: his son, 10-year-old John Quincy Adams, known to everyone as Johnny.

John Quincy Adams was the oldest son of future president John Adams and his wife Abigail. A precocious and well-educated child, John Quincy would grow up to be a lawyer and statesman, negotiating with foreign countries to ensure the expansion and independence of the United States.

The Adamses could not sail from Boston because spies were everywhere. Instead, father and son left home and went by sleigh to a nearby beach, where their ship, the *Boston,* waited offshore. They had been at sea for only two days when three British ships caught sight of the *Boston* and began following it. Two ships soon gave up, but the other kept after the *Boston* for three days until a fierce storm finally brought an end to the chase.

A bolt of lightning struck the *Boston*'s main mast, and a sailor was killed. The sea was so rough that Johnny and his father struggled to keep from falling out of bed, and both of them were seasick. The seas eventually calmed down, but their adventure was not over yet. Later in the voyage, they met another British ship, the *Martha*. A battle broke out and a shot sailed right over John Adams's head, but the *Boston* managed to capture the British ship.

Meanwhile, Johnny impressed everyone on board. A passenger began teaching him French, and the ship's captain showed him how the compass worked and taught him the names of the sails. John Adams was very proud of his son. He wrote to Abigail that Johnny had shown great courage throughout the difficult voyage.

Father and son survived their first trip to Europe. Like his father, Johnny would grow up to be a lawyer who represented his country abroad as a diplomat. Both men eventually became minister to Great Britain and president of the United States. John Adams, the second president, occupied the White House from 1797 to 1801. John Quincy Adams served as the sixth president, from 1825 to 1829.

EARLY YEARS IN BRAINTREE AND BOSTON

John Quincy Adams was born on July 11, 1767, about 10 miles south of Boston in Braintree (now Quincy), Massachusetts. The Adamses' two-story house was a New

England saltbox, with a steeply sloped roof and wooden siding. John Adams had his law office in a room on the first floor. He had been born in a similar house next door. The two houses were part of a farm with more than 100 acres of land located about a mile from the Atlantic Ocean. John was a respected lawyer whose cases often took him away from home. His wife, Abigail, came from a well-known family of clergymen. Both of them took an active role in deciding how Johnny and his siblings would be brought up.

At the time of Johnny's birth, the start of the Revolutionary War (1775–1783) was still eight years away, but trouble was already brewing between Great Britain and its American colonies. In 1763, the Seven Years' War had come to an end with Britain defeating its old enemy, France. Known in America as the French and Indian War, it had left Britain with a huge debt. As a result, Britain began taxing the 13 American colonies.

In 1767, just 12 days before Johnny was born, the British Parliament created a new tax act. The Townshend Acts taxed tea, lead, glass, paint, and paper imported from Britain. In Boston, violence broke out against customs inspectors who enforced the act, and in 1768, British troops arrived to keep order. The British weren't the only ones who arrived in town that year. John Adams's legal business was growing, so he moved his family to a large rented house in Boston.

Abigail was in that house on the night of March 5, 1770, when she heard the sounds of a church bell ringing and gunfire. The noise woke up two-year-old Johnny and his four-year-old sister, Abigail, known as Nabby. What they had heard was the sound of the Boston Massacre. Believing they were about to be attacked, British soldiers had fired into a crowd, killing five people and wounding six others.

In 1771, John moved the family back to Braintree, but two years later they returned to Boston. In December 1773, colonists dumped tea in Boston Harbor to protest the tax on tea, an event called the Boston Tea Party. In response to this, Britain closed the port of Boston and sent more troops. Life was getting dangerous in Boston. By now, John and Abigail had four children: Nabby, Johnny, Charles (born in 1770), and Thomas (born in 1772). John decided once again to move his family back to Braintree. At the end of the summer of 1774, he rode off to Philadelphia to attend the First Continental Congress.

THE REVOLUTIONARY WAR BEGINS

John Adams was in Braintree when the first shots of the Revolutionary War were fired at Lexington and Concord, Massachusetts, on April 19, 1775. A week later, he left for the Second Continental Congress in Philadelphia. The representatives present at this meeting elected George Washington to lead the Continental Army in the battle for independence. On the morning of June 17, the sound of booming cannons woke Abigail. Taking seven-year-old Johnny by the hand, she walked to the top of nearby Penn's Hill. From there, they could see Boston and the first major battle of the Revolutionary War, the Battle of Bunker Hill.

John Quincy was born in the family's saltbox house in Braintree, Massachusetts, outside Boston, on July 11, 1767. The family was there when the Revolutionary War broke out in 1775. Johnny, as he was known in younger years, and his mother walked to the top of a hill and watched the Battle of Bunker Hill, the first major battle of the war.

Johnny and his mother cried when they later found out that a family friend, Dr. Joseph Warren, had been killed in the battle. When Johnny had broken his finger, Dr. Warren had saved it from amputation.

The war came right to the Adamses' door. Families fleeing Boston stopped for food. Abigail took them in and let them stay a night or even a week. American militiamen marched past the house and drilled in a field on the farm.

Abigail gave them food, as well. Johnny watched as his mother and an uncle worked at the fireplace, melting down her pewter spoons for bullets. Abigail and her neighbors feared that the British would invade Braintree. John advised her to take the children and "fly to the woods" if that happened.

In early March 1776, George Washington and his American troops put cannons on Dorchester Heights and began to bombard the British in Boston. On March 17, Abigail climbed Penn's Hill again with Johnny and Nabby. This time, they watched as the British fleet sailed out of Boston Harbor. Washington had driven the British out of Boston, but the war was far from over.

EDUCATION FOR A LIFE OF PUBLIC SERVICE

From the time he was nine years old, Johnny rode a horse into Boston six days a week to pick up and deliver the family's mail. Abigail read John's letters from the Second Continental Congress in Philadelphia to the children. Some delegates at the Congress held out hope that the colonies could reach an agreement with Great Britain, but John Adams led the movement for independence. The whole family knew that he was playing an important role in the country's history. Johnny's parents expected that one day he would do great things, as well.

Johnny liked books and read more widely than most children his age. His father's law clerk was his first teacher, but when the clerk was called away by the war, Abigail took over. In August 1777, John Adams wrote to Johnny telling him that he must study Greek, Latin, and history to prepare himself for a life of public service. Earlier in the summer, Johnny had written to his father in Philadelphia and admitted, "my thoughts are running after birds' eggs, play and trifles." Then he asked for help in setting up a schedule for play and study.

> *"I wish, sir, you would give me some instructions with regard to my time, and advise me how to proportion my studies and my play, in writing, and I will keep them by me and endeavor to follow them."*
>
> — John Quincy Adams, in a letter to John Adams, June 2, 1777

Throughout his life, Johnny would always worry that he was wasting time instead of working.

A STUDENT ABROAD

When the Adamses arrived in Paris in 1778, after their perilous voyage on the *Boston*, John immediately enrolled Johnny in a French school. His French improved rapidly, leading John to write to Abigail that their son "learned more French in a day than I could learn in a week with all my books."

By the time they reached France, the country had already agreed to help the United States. There was still work for John to do as one of three American commissioners in Paris, so he and Johnny stayed in France for about a year. They sailed for the United States in June 1779. Their fellow passengers included the new French minister, or ambassador, to the United States and his secretary. Unfortunately, they did not speak much English. They soon found a tutor: 12-year-old Johnny. Apparently, he was a strict teacher: The secretary said that Johnny "shows us no mercy, and makes us no compliments."

On August 2, 1779, father and son arrived in Braintree. They remained at home for only three months. Congress wanted John Adams to return to France to negotiate peace and trade treaties with Britain. Johnny hoped to attend Andover Academy to prepare for Harvard College, but Abigail insisted that he accompany his father because the trip would be another chance to improve his education. This time, Johnny's younger brother Charles also went along.

It was on this trip that Johnny began writing in his diary, a habit he continued for the rest of his life. The resulting diary was enormous. Years after his death, his son published 12 volumes, which was only part of it. Johnny's first entries were about the voyage. Once again, the Adamses had bad luck at sea. "The ship is very leaky," he wrote. "The passengers are all called to the Pump four times a day."

A YOUNG MAN'S TRAVELS

The Adamses stayed in Paris for about six months. In the summer of 1780, they moved on to the Dutch Republic, also known as Holland or the Netherlands. John Adams wasn't satisfied with the French as allies and thought that the United States should seek help from another nation. He enrolled the boys in the Latin School in Amsterdam. Unable to speak Dutch, they were put in a class with younger students. Johnny was miserable there and began to misbehave, so John sent his sons to the University of Leyden, where Johnny was much happier. Charles, however, was in poor health and missed his mother. He eventually returned to the United States in 1782.

In the summer of 1781, Johnny went on his first mission for his country. Francis Dana, a member of John Adams's staff, was being sent to St. Petersburg, Russia, 2,000 miles away. Dana didn't speak French, the official language used at the court of Empress Catherine the Great. Johnny, who was just 14, would serve as his translator and private secretary. The plan was for Dana to persuade Catherine to recognize the United States as an independent country and then use Russia's power to influence other countries to do the same. Catherine, however, refused to deal with Dana, so there was little for Johnny to do.

John Adams assumed that Johnny would be able to continue his education in Russia, but Johnny soon found that there was no school for him to attend. All the rich people sent their children to Western Europe, and the poor didn't bother to educate their children. He did the best he could by reading on his own. Years later, he complained that his education in Europe had been too casual and more likely "to make me acquainted with men than books." Historians would disagree, arguing that his time spent traveling through Europe and talking with foreign ministers was the perfect education for a future diplomat. On the personal

Johnny's first diplomatic mission for the United States came in 1781 when he accompanied Francis Dana (pictured here), a member of John Adams's European staff, to Russia as a translator. Dana did not speak French—the official language of the Russian court—but Johnny spoke it fluently. Dana wanted to persuade Catherine the Great to recognize the United States as a separate country, thus furthering the independence movement.

side, Johnny's years in Europe left him with a lifelong love of the theater and bookstores.

Johnny left St. Petersburg to work as his father's private secretary. He traveled back to Holland at a leisurely pace, stopping in several countries and enjoying being independent of his parents. By the time father and son were reunited in July 1783, they hadn't seen each other for two years. At this time, Johnny helped his father prepare the papers for the Treaty of Paris, which officially ended the American Revolution in September 1783.

Johnny spent the next two years with his family in Paris. Abigail and Nabby also came to live in France, but Charles and Thomas stayed with relatives in Massachusetts. Johnny spent his time studying, going to the theater, and dining with friends such as Thomas Jefferson, the author of the Declaration of Independence. He often borrowed books from Jefferson, and John Adams later said that Jefferson was like a second father to his son.

> *"Spent the evening with Mr. Jefferson whom I love to be with because he is a man of very extensive learning and pleasing manners."*
>
> — John Quincy Adams, in his diary, March 11, 1785

In April 1785, John Adams was notified that Congress had appointed him the first U.S. minister to Great Britain. Johnny didn't want to go along, and Abigail thought he needed to start thinking about earning a living. It was time for Johnny to enroll at Harvard College.

2

LAWYER AND DIPLOMAT

A FEW DAYS after his eighteenth birthday in July 1785, John Quincy Adams arrived in New York City, which was then the capital of the United States. He had just sailed from France, so everyone wanted to hear his opinions and the latest news from Europe. Johnny dined with New York businessmen, U.S. congressmen, and foreign diplomats. He stayed for a month before heading home to Braintree. His relatives were impressed with the intelligent, well-spoken young man that he had become. In fact, it seemed that everyone was impressed with him—everyone, that is, except Joseph Willard, the president of Harvard.

On August 31, Johnny met with Willard at the college in

Harvard College, shown here in the eighteenth century, was the most prestigious university in the United States. Joseph Willard, the president of the college in 1785, did not think that Johnny's Latin and Greek were up to Harvard's standard. Although he had studied at a famous European school, Johnny had to be tutored in order to gain admittance to the college.

Cambridge, Massachusetts. He expected to sail through his entrance exam—after all, he had studied at the world-famous University of Leyden. Now the president of this small college, which didn't even have a decent library, was refusing to admit him. Willard felt that Johnny needed to be tutored in Latin and Greek. He recommended Reverend John Shaw, a minister living in Haverhill, Massachusetts.

Johnny was terribly embarrassed that he needed a tutor, but he soon was on his way to Haverhill.

Reverend Shaw was Johnny's uncle, married to Abigail Adams's sister, Elizabeth. Johnny spent six months with the Shaws. He studied, went to church twice on Sundays, and began to socialize with people his own age. In March 1786, Johnny appeared before President Willard again. This time he was admitted to Harvard as a junior or third-year student.

The busiest days of his week were Monday and Wednesday. Here is the schedule he shared with his classmates on May 3, 1786: Beginning at six A.M., the students went to prayers and then recited. After breakfast, they had a divinity or religion lecture, followed by a lecture on levers and pulleys. After lunch, there was a lecture on the planet Mercury, more reciting, and, finally, prayers at five P.M.

There was more to Harvard than lectures and studying. Johnny liked to spend time talking with friends, and he also began playing the flute. Other Harvard students got drunk and broke windows, but Johnny's worst offense was oversleeping and being late for prayers. For that, he was fined a penny.

After less than a year and a half, on July 18, 1787, Johnny graduated from Harvard with a bachelor of arts degree. He ranked second in his class of 51 and gave a speech, "Upon the Importance and Necessity of Public Faith, to the Well-Being of a Community," at graduation. The Boston newspapers didn't think much of it, expecting more from the son of a diplomat who had been educated in Europe. One hundred guests came to Johnny's graduation dinner. Four hundred more showed up for dessert, which included a plum cake made from 24 pounds of flour. On a personal note, the new graduate decided to start using John instead of his childhood nickname, Johnny.

STUDYING LAW IN NEWBURYPORT

John Quincy's parents missed his graduation because John Adams was still serving as minister to Great Britain. Nonetheless, they continued to influence him from across the ocean. John and Abigail insisted that he become a lawyer. John Quincy didn't like that idea, but he agreed to their plan anyway. How else could he earn a living?

In September 1787, he traveled to Newburyport, about 40 miles north of Boston, to begin studying law with Theophilus Parsons. A well-known lawyer, Parsons later became chief justice of the Massachusetts Supreme Court.

When he wasn't studying, Adams and his fellow apprentices led an active social life. His diary is full of comments about the young ladies of Newburyport. There were sleighing parties, dances, and even kissing games, although Adams didn't think much of kissing someone he didn't like. More than

> "The question, what am I to do in this world recurs to me, very frequently; and never without causing great anxiety, and a depression of spirits: my prospects appear darker to me, every day, and I am obliged sometimes to drive the subject from my mind, and to assume some more agreeable train of thoughts."
> — John Quincy Adams, in his diary, December 18, 1787

once, he didn't come home until four A.M. Despite all this activity, he was unhappy in Newburyport from the beginning and constantly worried about his future. By October 1788, he was so depressed that he went home to Braintree for five months.

The next year, 1789, would prove to be a better year for him. In the spring, George Washington became the first president of the United States, with John Adams as his vice president. By that summer, John Quincy was in love. Like many men of his time, John Quincy thought women were inferior to men. At age 22, however, he suddenly fell in love with Mary Frazier, a pretty, blonde 15-year-old.

A BOSTON LAWYER AND POLITICAL WRITER

On July 15, 1790, John Quincy Adams was sworn in as a lawyer. He hoped to stay in Newburyport to be near Mary, but his parents insisted that he would have more opportunities for work if he set up an office in Boston. Abigail also said it was wrong for him to be carrying on a romance when he couldn't support a wife. John Quincy wanted Mary to agree to marry him without setting a wedding date, but her family insisted on a formal engagement. Reluctantly, in November 1790, the couple decided to break up. Many years later, Adams said it took him four years to get over her.

Life in Boston did not go well for Adams. He lost his first case, and he didn't have any money, so he had to live with relatives. His father was still sending him an allowance. He was depressed and bored and felt that other men his age were getting ahead of him in the world. Then he read *The Rights of Man* by Thomas Paine and his life changed. He began to get involved in politics.

The French Revolution had started in 1789, and Paine argued that Great Britain should follow France's example and overthrow its king. John Quincy disagreed. He didn't like the idea of angry mobs of people determining what an entire country should do. He was also upset by some words of praise that Thomas Jefferson had written for Paine's work. Although Jefferson didn't mention anyone by name, he accused some leaders of the American Revolution of being traitors to their original ideals. John Quincy took this as an attack on his father.

In response, John Quincy wrote a series of letters under the name of Publicola. They were published in a Boston newspaper during the summer of 1791. Some people thought that John Adams was Publicola, but others realized that the letters were too well written to be his work.

> *"This principle, that a whole nation has a right to do whatever it pleases, cannot in any sense whatever be admitted as true."*
>
> — John Quincy Adams, "Letters of Publicola," 1791

They were reprinted in Europe, and John Quincy began receiving attention for his writing.

He also started working in local politics, both in Boston and in Braintree. He drafted the necessary papers when people in the northern part of Braintree

Early in the nation's history, Thomas Jefferson was a great friend of the Adams family. Johnny was disappointed when Jefferson endorsed some of the actions of revolutionaries during the French Revolution. Jefferson believed that some of the leaders of the American independence movement, including John Adams, had abandoned their original ideals.

wanted to create a separate town. The new town was named Quincy, after his great-grandfather, John Quincy—the same person he had been named after.

In 1793 and early 1794, John Quincy published more essays using the names Marcellus, Columbus, and Barneveld. By this time, France was fighting Great Britain and much of Europe in the Wars of the French Revolution (1792–1800). President Washington thought that the United States should remain neutral and not take sides. John Quincy's essays supported the president. Washington took note of the young essayist and would soon reward him.

John Quincy enjoyed writing, and for the rest of his life, he would be torn between the desire to be a great writer or a politician. It was clear which path his father wanted him to take. In a letter, John reminded John Quincy that he was born with many advantages and that if he didn't rise to the head of the legal profession and become president of the United States, it was his own fault. To his wife, John Adams wrote, "All my hopes are in him, both for my family and my country."

MINISTER TO THE NETHERLANDS

In 1794, George Washington gave John Quincy the chance to serve his country as minister to the Netherlands. His parents were delighted. Now he would be launched on the life of public service that they had always envisioned for him. John Quincy was not so happy. He didn't want to leave Boston, but more important, he didn't think that he was qualified for the job. He worried that Washington had only chosen him because he was John Adams's son.

Once he arrived in the Netherlands, there wasn't much for him to do. He did have one important job: to report back to the United States on what was happening in Europe. He kept in touch with the ministers at the four other American embassies in London, Paris, Lisbon, and Madrid. He soon realized that he liked being a diplomat because he had the best of both worlds: He was involved with politics, but he also had plenty of free time to pursue his own reading and writing.

In November 1795, he was sent to London to handle the final exchange of papers for the Jay Treaty, which settled violations of the Treaty of Paris and regulated trade between Great Britain and the United States. Bad weather made his ship late, so by the time he arrived, everything was done. John Quincy stayed in London for six months, spending most of his time courting Louisa Catherine Johnson. When Abigail learned of his new romance, she tried to interfere again. She knew the Johnson family from her time in London and didn't approve of them. Louisa was a beautiful and intelligent woman, who could be as stubborn as John Quincy. When he returned to the Netherlands in the spring of 1796, they were engaged, but he refused to set a wedding date. President Washington made him minister to Portugal, and Louisa was determined to marry him before he left. They were married on July 26, 1797, but they did not go to Portugal.

A NEW PRESIDENT AND
A NEW MINISTER TO PRUSSIA

As of March 1797, the United States had a new president: John Adams. He appointed his son to be the first U.S. minister to Prussia, part of modern Germany. Just days before he married Louisa in London, John Quincy received a letter telling him the news. He was upset. Once again, it looked as if he had gotten an appointment because of his father.

Shortly after the Adamses arrived in Berlin, Louisa had a miscarriage. Over the next two years, she would lose three more babies. On April 12, 1801, Louisa finally gave birth to a son, George Washington Adams.

Aside from working on renewing a U.S. treaty with Prussia, there wasn't much for John Quincy to do during his four years as minister. He studied German and began translating some books into English. He also began to think of translating as a new career. Politics at home, however, interfered with his life as a man of letters.

In the presidential election of 1800, John Adams was defeated by Thomas Jefferson. In the years since the men were in France together, they had become enemies as two political parties formed in the United States. Adams represented the Federalists, who wanted a strong central government and closer ties with Great Britain. Jefferson led the Democratic-Republicans, who thought the states

John Adams became the second president of the United States in March 1797. He soon appointed his son to the new position of U.S. minister to Prussia. John Quincy felt that as before, he only received a position because of his father's power in the government.

should have more control than the federal government and that France would be a better ally than Britain. In the election of 1796, Jefferson had finished in second place and, according to election rules of that time, he became Adams's vice president. The two men rarely worked together.

Now, in 1801, John Adams did not want to give Jefferson the satisfaction of replacing his son as minister. As one of his final acts in office, he signed the papers ordering John Quincy to leave Prussia. John Quincy had spent seven years in Europe. Once again, it was time to go home. What would he do once he got there?

3

AN INDEPENDENT SENATOR AND DIPLOMAT

IN 1801, THE Adams family was mourning more than John's loss of the White House. John Quincy's brother Charles had died on November 30, 1800, at the age of 30. Alcohol had contributed to his death, making Abigail Adams's worst fear come true. She had always worried that her sons would turn out like her brother, William Smith, who had abandoned his family and died an alcoholic. This was one reason that she constantly pushed John Quincy to succeed. Now, in the fall of 1801, John Quincy was back in Massachusetts without a job.

Politics seemed out of the question. Everybody in the family was bitter about John Adams's defeat. "If I were to go over my life

John Quincy Adams never truly desired to enter politics, especially after his father's disappointing loss to Thomas Jefferson in the presidential election of 1800. Still, the Federalist Party asked him to run for office and he accepted. John Quincy was elected to the United States Senate in 1803, eight years after this 1795 portrait was completed.

again," the former president said, "I would be a shoemaker rather than an American statesman." John Quincy himself said he'd rather clean filth from the streets than enter politics. Neither father nor son liked the fact that political parties had become so powerful. Trying to console his father over the election loss, John Quincy told him, "in your administration you were the man not of any party, but of the whole nation. . . ." Those are important words because when he was later elected to office, John Quincy refused to be bound by the wishes of his party.

John Quincy returned to being a lawyer in Boston, but within a few months, he was a candidate for office. The Federalist Party asked him to run for the Massachusetts State Senate. He won the election and took office in May 1802. Why did he change his mind about a career in politics? Perhaps it was because he hated being a lawyer. Or perhaps it was because on some level, he actually enjoyed politics, viewing himself as a statesman who could make a difference in the world. The Federalists soon found that they couldn't control their newest senator: He voted the way he wanted to, even if it meant going against his own party.

UNITED STATES SENATOR

In 1803, John Quincy was elected to the United States Senate. That same year, France had agreed to sell the Louisiana Territory to the United States, doubling the size of the country. The New England Federalists opposed the Louisiana Purchase, fearing that they would lose power as more states entered the Union in the West. John Quincy was in favor of the purchase, seeing it as a chance for the United States to become a great nation. He was very disappointed when he arrived in Washington, D.C., too late to vote in favor of the purchase. His wife had become ill during the trip from Massachusetts, delaying their arrival.

Adams came to Washington with Louisa, son George, and a new baby, John II, who was born on July 4, 1803. Washington was not yet a beautiful capital city. The streets were muddy, and there were no churches, so Adams had to attend religious services at either the Capitol or the Treasury office. He regularly walked two and a half miles to the Capitol for Senate sessions. The walk took 45 minutes, and he was often late. He also neglected his appearance, a bad habit he had had since his youth. In her letters, his mother reminded him to dress neatly. She didn't want people to think poorly of her because her son, the senator, looked sloppy.

He had another habit that the Federalists didn't approve of: He often dined at the White House with their political enemy, President Jefferson. He also annoyed his fellow senators by making amendments, or additions, that basically corrected grammar in bills. Adams went his own way in the Senate, voting as he saw fit and not caring if he offended the Federalists.

His troubles with his political party grew more serious in 1807. That June, the British ship the *Leopard* attacked the U.S. Navy ship the *Chesapeake* off the coast of Virginia. The British claimed that four of the *Chesapeake*'s men were deserters from the British navy. The four men were seized and killed. Since the 1790s, British ships had been stopping American merchant ships, supposedly looking for deserters that they could bring back into the navy. In reality, Britain needed men for its navy, and this was a way to get them. By 1815, the British had seized or impressed nearly 10,000 seamen, most of them American citizens.

Merchants in New England depended heavily on trade with Britain, so the Federalists tried to ignore the impressment issue. Adams, however, was outraged when the Federalists would not protest against the *Chesapeake* incident. He went to a rally held by the Democratic-Republicans and was put on a committee to draft resolutions against Britain. In November 1807, Adams wrote in his diary that he thought war was coming with Britain. He also complained that too many people were willing to do whatever Britain wanted just to avoid war.

Adams further angered the Federalists when he voted in favor of Jefferson's Embargo Act in December 1807. As the Napoleonic Wars (1800–1815) raged in Europe, an economic struggle also took place. Both France and Britain imposed severe restrictions on merchant ships coming from neutral countries such as the United States. Jefferson responded with the Embargo Act, which forced American ships to stay home. The idea was to make Britain and France realize how much they needed to trade with the United States and to make them respect the

> *"On most of the great national questions now under discussion, my sense of duty leads me to support the Administration, and I find myself of course in opposition to the federalists in general."*
>
> — John Quincy Adams, in his diary, December 31, 1807

rights of neutral countries. Instead, the act was an economic disaster, especially for New England. Adams helped write the Embargo Act and was the only Federalist to vote for it.

In January 1808, Adams went to a Democratic-Republican caucus, where members of Congress chose James Madison as their candidate for president. Adams received one vote for vice president. This was the end of Senator Adams as far as the Federalists were concerned. In those days, the state legislatures, not the public, elected U.S. senators. In June 1808, the Massachusetts legislature voted to replace Adams when his term ended the following year. Adams chose to resign a few days later.

Adams once again went back to being a lawyer. He also had another job as a professor at Harvard, which he had held since 1806. He taught rhetoric and oratory—what we would call public speaking. Adams's careers as a lawyer and professor would last only another year.

In March 1809, Adams went to Washington to argue two cases before the Supreme Court. He stopped off to visit the newly inaugurated President Madison. The president soon announced that he had an appointment for Adams: minister to Russia.

MINISTER TO RUSSIA

In August 1809, John Quincy and Louisa sailed for St. Petersburg, Russia, with their two-year-old son, Charles Francis, who had been born in 1807. They left George, age 8, and John, age 6, at home with relatives, a

John Quincy married Louisa Catherine Johnson on July 26, 1797.
Louisa was British and was never truly accepted by Americans
although her father was an American diplomat. Louisa Adams is still
the only First Lady born outside the United States.

decision that Louisa would always regret. It would be six
years before they were reunited with their sons in England.
There was an urgency to their travels, because they had to

reach St. Petersburg before Kronstadt harbor froze, cutting the city off from the rest of the world for the winter.

Adams quickly became friendly with Czar Alexander I, the ruler of Russia. Both men liked to walk, and they often ran into each other during their strolls. Alexander was surprised that Adams didn't wear gloves or mittens in the cold weather. He was also surprised to see Adams one day without his wig. Adams stopped wearing it altogether after the czar told him that he didn't need to wear it at court.

Once again, Adams's role was to let the president know what was happening in Europe. He also kept up with the news from America. In 1811, he wrote to his father that he felt that the United States would eventually occupy the whole continent. This was probably the most important theme of his political life. It lay behind his support of the Louisiana Purchase when he was a U.S. senator. It would be the basis for many of his decisions when he later became secretary of state.

"The whole continent of North America appears to be destined by Divine Providence to be peopled by one nation, speaking one language, professing one general system of religious and political principles, and accustomed to one general tenor of social usages and customs. For the common happiness of them all, for their peace and prosperity, I believe it indispensable that they should be associated in one federal Union."
— John Quincy Adams, in a letter to John Adams, August 31, 1811

Adams was offered a chance to come home in 1811. President Madison was planning to name him to the Supreme Court. Adams turned the job down, saying that his wife was pregnant and unable to travel. It is also possible that he declined the job because it paid less than he was making in Russia and he really didn't want to be a judge. His daughter, Louisa Catherine, was born on August 12, 1811.

While in Russia, Adams became more religious. He read the Bible every day and was able to do so in a variety of languages, including French, German, Latin, and Greek, as well as English. He also became interested in astronomy, even though his only magnifying tool was a pair of opera glasses. He used much of his time to pursue his own studies. Still, he was always unhappy with himself, writing in his diary at the end of each year that he hadn't accomplished enough.

The year 1812 was one of upheaval. The French emperor, Napoleon, invaded Russia, the United States declared war on Great Britain, and one-year-old Louisa Catherine died. For Adams and his wife, Louisa's death was the most devastating of the three events. Napoleon was soon sent scurrying out of Russia, defeated by lack of supplies and the weather, or, as Adams put it, by "*General Famine* and *General Frost.*" Czar Alexander offered to try to make peace between Great Britain and the United States to end the War of 1812, but the British didn't want his help.

PEACEMAKER

In August 1814, the British and the Americans began peace talks in Ghent, a city in what is now Belgium. Adams was the head of the five-man American delegation, which included Henry Clay, the former Speaker of the House of Representatives. At times, Adams could barely get along with the other men. He liked to wake up early, but they stayed up late, playing cards, drinking, and smoking cigars. He felt that they rewrote everything he wrote just for the sake of rewriting it. The Americans lost their tempers with each other and with the British.

> *"Mr. Clay is losing his temper and growing peevish and fractious. I, too, must not forget to keep a constant guard upon my temper, for the time is evidently approaching when it will be wanted."*
>
> — John Quincy Adams, in his diary, October 31, 1814

A number of issues, including the impressment of American sailors and the rights of ships from neutral countries to sail the seas, divided the Americans and the British. The Americans wanted to continue to have the right to fish off the Atlantic coast of Canada. The British wanted to set up a neutral zone between U.S. and British territory in the Northwest to be occupied by Native Americans. The British also wanted to control the Great Lakes and to be able to sail the Mississippi River, a major transportation route. Adams finally offered a simple solution that ended the war: Leave all these issues for future talks, and let everything go back to the way it was before the war. The British agreed, and both sides signed the Treaty of Ghent on December 24, 1814.

There was one more dispute to be settled, this one among members of the American negotiating team. Who would keep the papers, books, and maps that they

John Quincy Adams was instrumental in bringing the War of 1812, between Britain and the United States, to an end with the Treaty of Ghent. The signing of the treaty, captured in this 1914 painting, took place on December 24, 1814. The American delegation, which included Adams and Henry Clay, had many disputes among its members.

had used? Adams felt he had a right to them as head of the team. Henry Clay thought he should take them back to the State Department. They agreed to divide everything after Adams threatened to make an official report about their dispute.

Like his father, who negotiated the end of the American Revolution, John Quincy Adams had ended a war with Britain. Also like his father, he became minister to Great Britain, a position he held from 1815 to 1817. While in London, John Quincy settled one of the issues left unresolved at the end of the War of 1812: The British agreed to limit the size and number of warships on the Great Lakes.

The position of minister to Great Britain was viewed as the highest diplomatic post abroad, but there were rumors that Adams would receive an even more important appointment. In 1817, James Monroe became the fifth president of the United States and named Adams as his secretary of state. Adams had been away from home for eight years, and during that period, his sister, Nabby, had died from cancer. This time, Adams was returning to the United States to stay. The coming years would bring him many professional triumphs and personal sorrows.

SECRETARY
OF STATE

WHEN JOHN QUINCY ADAMS arrived in Washington, D.C., in September 1817, he found the State Department in chaos. Important papers were missing, and the filing system was a mess. It was difficult to get any work done because he had so many visitors. Members of the House of Representatives and Senate hung around his office asking for favors for the people in their home states. Adams soon realized he could avoid many of them if he came to work after Congress was in session for the day.

As secretary of state, he was the member of President Monroe's cabinet in charge of relations with foreign governments. He had other duties, too. He supervised the Patent Office and the census.

Henry Clay, the Speaker of the House of Representatives, was one of the candidates for the presidency in 1824. He had expected to become secretary of state under President James Monroe, but John Quincy Adams received the appointment instead.

Congress asked him to prepare a report on weights and measures. This was a project that truly captured Adams's interest because it involved so many subjects: math, science, history, and philosophy. He came to admire the metric system that Napoleon had imposed upon Europe. He spent more than three years working on the report between other duties, and he thought the final paper one of his best. Congress never took any action on his recommendations.

LOOKING FORWARD TO THE PRESIDENCY

Because Adams was secretary of state, it was widely assumed that he would be the next president of the United States. Three former secretaries of state—Thomas Jefferson, James Madison, and James Monroe—had gone on to the presidency. As a result, all the other men in Washington who wanted to be president went out of their way to make life difficult for Adams and to criticize him. Sitting in the cabinet were two men with their eyes on the White House: John C. Calhoun, the secretary of war, and William H. Crawford, the secretary of the treasury. Crawford was especially bitter because he had lost the Democratic-Republican Party's presidential nomination to Monroe in 1816.

Another enemy was Henry Clay, who was once again the Speaker of the House of Representatives. He had expected to become secretary of state and was disappointed when Adams received the position. Clay came from Kentucky, one of the western states, and Adams thought he was trying to organize the West against the Monroe administration.

Many people assumed that Monroe would win the presidency again in 1820. Thus far, John Adams was the only president not elected to a second term. John Quincy Adams's political rivals were therefore looking ahead to the campaign of 1824. Adams's friends urged him to show some interest in running, but he refused. He said that he had never sought public office in the past and he was not going to start now. If people wanted him to be president, they would have to ask him to run.

Adams realized that if he did decide to run for president, his prickly personality could work against him. "I well know that I never was and never shall be what is commonly termed a popular man," he wrote to his wife in 1821. His friends encouraged him to go out more so that people could get to know him, but he felt that his time was better spent at home, reading and writing.

> "I never, by the most distant hint to any one, expressed a wish for any public office, and I should not now begin to ask for that which of all others ought to be most freely and spontaneously bestowed."
>
> — John Quincy Adams, in his diary, March 18, 1818

Traditionally, members of the cabinet and their wives had called on all the new members of Congress. The Adamses thought this was a waste of time. They stuck to their policy, even after President Monroe and his wife, Elizabeth, spoke to them about it. Adams did his best to ignore the gossip and campaign talk so that he could do the real work of the State Department: negotiating with foreign governments.

AN AGREEMENT WITH GREAT BRITAIN

Adams had helped negotiate the Treaty of Ghent, which ended the War of 1812. That treaty left a number of issues between Great Britain and the United States unresolved. In 1818, negotiators from both sides met in London to settle some of these issues. The Americans were guided by instructions that Adams had drawn up. The resulting agreement, called the Convention of 1818, settled the boundary between the United States and Canada. The two sides agreed that the 49th parallel, or the imaginary line at 49 degrees north latitude, would be the boundary from Minnesota west to the Rocky Mountains. The two countries would jointly occupy the area from the Rockies to the Pacific, with this part of the agreement to be renewed every ten years.

The fishing problem was also resolved. Great Britain agreed that U.S. fishermen could continue to fish off the coast of eastern Canada. The two sides also decided to have a neutral party resolve one other issue: whether the British should pay American slave-owners for slaves who had been taken during the war. This issue was later resolved in favor of the slave-owners.

The Convention of 1818 was signed in October. That same month, Adams's mother, Abigail, died at the age of 73. He did not go home to Quincy, saying that he was too busy with State Department business.

TROUBLE IN FLORIDA

Great Britain was not the only country that claimed territory in North America: Spain also had settlements. The United States owned western Florida, and Spain claimed the rest. With British help, Spain was encouraging the Seminole Indians to attack U.S. citizens in Georgia. After the attacks, the Seminole warriors retreated to safety in Florida. President Monroe sent General Andrew Jackson to handle the conflict, part of the First Seminole War (1817–1818).

Jackson swept through Florida, killing Seminoles and seizing two Spanish military posts. He also executed the two British soldiers behind the attacks. Many people thought that Jackson had gone well beyond what Monroe had authorized him to do, and both Great Britain and Spain demanded that he be punished. Adams was the only man in Monroe's cabinet who thought that Jackson had acted properly. He said that if Spain could not keep the Seminoles from attacking American citizens, it shouldn't have colonies.

Monroe decided not to punish Jackson. Instead he assigned Adams to try to purchase Florida for the United States. In February 1819, Adams sat down with Spain's minister, Luis de Onis. Spain agreed to sell Florida to the United States for $5 million. The two men also settled a long-standing border question. The western edge of the Louisiana Purchase had never been agreed upon. Spain wanted the Mississippi River to be the borderline. Americans wanted it to extend at least into Texas. Under the Adams–Onis Treaty, also called the Transcontinental Treaty of 1819, the border started at the Gulf of Mexico and ran north along the Sabine River, the border between modern Texas and Louisiana. The border then went northwest, following rivers and extending to the Pacific Ocean along the 42nd parallel, the southern border of what are now Oregon and Idaho. Spain would

> *"I considered the signature of the [Adams–Onis] treaty as the most important event of my life. It was an event of magnitude in the history of this Union."*
>
> — John Quincy Adams, in his diary, February 22, 1821

The Adams–Onis Treaty, written by John Quincy Adams and Spain's minister, Luis de Onis, purchased the Florida Territory for the United States for $5 million and resolved the question over the western border of the Louisiana Territory, purchased for the United States in 1803 by Thomas Jefferson.

own the land south and west of this new border. As part of the treaty, Spain also agreed to abandon its claims to Oregon. In return, the United States agreed to give up its claims to Texas. Critics in both countries felt that their side had given up too much land. Adams, on the other hand, thought that his negotiations had accomplished something great for the United States, extending its border to the Pacific.

Unfortunately for Adams, Henry Clay found a mistake in the treaty. Because of an incorrect date, two large sections of Florida would still belong to Spain. Clay did not keep quiet about the error—after all, he wanted to be president, and here was a chance to embarrass Adams. Onis agreed to fix the date, but Adams had to wait a long time for the Spanish government to sign the treaty.

THE MONROE DOCTRINE

Meanwhile, Spain's colonies in Latin America had declared their independence. Clay urged President Monroe to recognize them as new nations, but Adams was more cautious. He feared that Spain would not ratify the Adams–Onis Treaty if the United States recognized the Latin American countries. The Spanish government finally ratified the treaty in 1821. President Monroe asked Congress to recognize the Latin American nations in 1822, and the United States became the first nation to do so.

There was talk, however, that Spain might try to reclaim its former colonies with the help of the Holy Alliance, made up of France, Russia, Prussia, and Austria. Great Britain, however, had been trading with the Latin American countries and did not want to see Spain back in control. The British government therefore suggested that the United States join it in issuing a statement warning the Holy Alliance to stay out of the Americas. President Monroe asked former presidents Jefferson and Madison for advice. They approved of the British idea, but Adams did not. He persuaded Monroe and the cabinet that it was better for the United States to stand up for itself and make its own statement.

That statement was contained in Monroe's Seventh

Annual Message to Congress, delivered on December 2, 1823. A president's annual message was similar to today's State of the Union address except that the president did not read it aloud. In Monroe's annual message, hidden among reports on the state of the post office and an outbreak of illness at a military base, were the words that would later become known as the Monroe Doctrine. Although history has given the credit to Monroe, Adams was really the man behind the message.

The Monroe Doctrine stated that the United States had never interfered in European affairs. Europe, therefore,

PRESIDENT JOHN QUINCY ADAMS'S LEGACY

Secretary of State

Many historians regard John Quincy Adams as the greatest secretary of state in American history. A large expanse of land didn't have to be occupied by only one nation—Adams had only to look at Europe, the continent he knew best, to see that. He envisioned the United States as a big country, running from the Atlantic to the Pacific. With the Convention of 1818 and the Adams–Onis Treaty of 1819, he ensured that the United States would be a transcontinental nation.

Perhaps even more important, he saw the United States as a major power in the world. Other political leaders had expressed the two main ideas of the Monroe Doctrine—no more colonization and no interference with governments in the Americas—but it was Adams who made these ideas official government policy. In turning down Britain's offer to make a joint statement to Europe, the United States showed that it could stand up for itself. Presidents from John Tyler (1841–1845) to Theodore Roosevelt (1901–1909) to Ronald Reagan (1981–1989) have used the Monroe Doctrine as the basis for their actions.

should not interfere with the governments in North and South America. It also declared, "the American continents, by the free and independent condition which they have assumed and maintain, are henceforth not to be considered as subjects for future colonization by any European powers."

The declaration that there would be no more colonies was also a warning to Russia. That country had claimed territory along the west coast of North America as far south as Oregon. Adams persuaded Russia to sign the Treaty of 1824, agreeing not to establish settlements south of what is now Alaska.

Despite his successes in the diplomatic world, Adams longed for a life of reading and writing. He was always writing poetry, and he was especially pleased to be elected president of the American Academy of Arts and Sciences in 1820. He was disappointed that his three sons showed little interest in learning. One year he refused to let John and Charles come to Washington for Christmas vacation because they weren't doing well at Harvard. He insisted that they stay in Quincy and study with their grandfather, the former president. The previous year, all three boys had been home for Christmas, and Adams read aloud "Messiah" by British poet Alexander Pope. He later complained in his diary that only George had paid any attention. "Literature has been the charm of my life," he wrote, "and, could I have carved out my own fortunes, to literature would my whole life have been devoted. I have been a lawyer for bread, and a statesman at the call of my country."

In 1824, his country called him to the presidency.

5

PRESIDENT OF THE UNITED STATES

BY DECEMBER OF 1823, John Quincy Adams had decided that he did want to run for president. With Louisa's help, he began planning a special ball to honor Andrew Jackson. A popular figure from Tennessee, Jackson had briefly served in both the U.S. House and Senate in the 1790s. He was best known as the hero of the Battle of New Orleans in the War of 1812.

Adams had been the only man in President Monroe's cabinet to defend Jackson's military actions in Florida during the First Seminole War (1817–1818). Monroe later made Jackson governor of the Florida Territory. Jackson's actions in Florida helped to make him even more popular, especially in the western states. The

Louisa and John Quincy Adams held a ball in honor of Andrew Jackson in January 1824. Jackson (center) was the hero of the Battle of New Orleans in the War of 1812 and had been governor of the Florida Territory. Adams (far right) wanted Jackson's support for his presidential run and also to persuade Jackson to run as his vice president. Unfortunately for Adams, Jackson decided to run for president instead.

Tennessee legislature nominated him for president in 1822, two years before the next election. His political backers thought that he needed more time in the national spotlight, so a year later, the state legislature made him a U.S. senator. Jackson arrived in Washington in early December

1823. A little more than a month later, he was at the Adamses' house, attending the ball in his honor.

The purpose of the ball was to celebrate the anniversary of the Battle of New Orleans. Adams, however, had another motive. He knew that Jackson would be a strong contender for president. If Adams were going to win, he needed Jackson on his ticket to bring in votes from the western states. On the night of the ball, a thousand people crowded into the Adams home. Louisa Adams took General Jackson's arm and walked from room to room, introducing the new senator. To many guests, an Adams–Jackson ticket seemed likely. Jackson, though, wanted to be president, not Adams's vice president.

THE ELECTION OF 1824

Today, primary elections and special meetings called caucuses help political parties determine who will be their candidates. Any eligible voter can vote in a primary or attend a caucus. This process was much different in the early nineteenth century, when a group of congressmen from each party chose the candidates in secret caucuses. The Democratic-Republicans called a caucus for February 1824. By this point, the Federalist Party was almost dead, and Adams had long since broken with it anyway. Whoever won this caucus would probably be the next president, because all of the candidates were Democratic-Republicans.

Some people objected to the caucus system because it was secretive and didn't give the people a chance to be involved. Few congressmen attended the caucus, which nominated William H. Crawford, secretary of the treasury. Adams and Jackson paid no attention to the results. Neither did Henry Clay, Speaker of the House, who was also running for president. Adams's other rival in the cabinet, Secretary of War John C. Calhoun, soon realized that he would have a better chance as a vice-presidential candidate.

The 1824 election was the first one to compile a national total for the popular vote, the number of votes cast by the people. Jackson was the winner with 152,901 votes. Adams came in second with 114,023 votes. Crawford and Clay each had about 47,000 votes. The election was not over yet. According to the Constitution, the winner was not determined by the popular vote but by the electoral college. Each state had the same number of electors as it had representatives and senators in Congress. In 1824, six states used their legislatures to choose electors. When men voted in the other 16 states, they were actually voting for electors, who pledged to vote for the candidate of their party.

In the electoral college, Jackson received 99 votes, Adams 84, Crawford 41, and Clay 37. Jackson had won the most votes, but the Constitution required him to have an absolute majority, or at least one vote over half the total. He needed 32 more votes. Therefore, members of the U.S. House of Representatives would decide the election. Under the Twelfth Amendment to the Constitution, the House would choose from among the top three finishers, so Clay was out of the race.

Clay had won the votes of three western states in the

electoral college: Kentucky, Missouri, and Ohio. Who would get those votes now? Crawford had been disabled by a stroke, so Clay had to choose between Adams and Jackson. For Clay, Adams represented the lesser of two evils. Like Clay, he favored a strong national bank and high tariffs that protected American manufactured goods from European competition. Both men thought that the federal government should undertake a vast program of public works such as highways and canals. On January 9, 1825, Adams wrote in his diary: "Mr. Clay came at six, and spent the evening with me in a long conversation explanatory of the past and prospective of the future." Clay promised his electoral votes to Adams.

The House was scheduled to vote on February 9, 1825. Some people expected that it would take days to settle the election because that's what had happened the last time the House had chosen the president. That was in the election of 1800, when Thomas Jefferson defeated John Adams.

According to the Constitution, members of the House voted by state. Each state had one vote. The winner needed votes from at least 13 states to have an absolute majority of the 24 states. It took only one ballot for Adams to win the election. He received 13 votes. Jackson had 7 votes and Crawford won 4. On that day, Jackson became the first man to win the popular vote but lose the White House.

Soon after he won, Adams announced that Henry Clay would be his secretary of state. Jackson was out-raged. He accused Adams of giving Clay the job as a reward for securing Adams's election to the presidency. "Was there ever witnessed such a bare faced corruption in any country before?" he shouted. Voters in the western states were angry too. They felt that Clay had bargained their votes for the cabinet post. Jackson's supporters took up the cry of "corrupt bargain." It didn't matter whether Adams and Clay had really made a deal or not: To many people, it *looked* as if they had.

> *"Fellow-citizens, you are acquainted with the peculiar circumstances of the recent election. . . . Less possessed of your confidence in advance than any of my predecessors, I am deeply conscious of the prospect that I shall stand more and oftener in need of your indulgence."*
> — John Quincy Adams,
> in his inaugural address,
> March 4, 1825

AN INEFFECTIVE PRESIDENT

From the time he was a child, Adams had been groomed to be president. He was an intelligent man with many ideas for improving his country and should have been a great president. Instead he was able to accomplish little, and the presidency was one of the low points of his life. The Jackson-controlled Congress worked against him, and the "corrupt bargain" charge followed him everywhere. Adams didn't do much to help himself. Traditionally, presidents replaced federal jobholders with their own men, but if someone was qualified for the job, Adams kept him no matter what his political leanings. For example, Adams refused to fire the postmaster general, who was working against

John Quincy Adams became the sixth president of the United States through a process that was more complicated than most elections. Jackson won the most votes in the electoral college, but he did not have an absolute majority. The House of Representatives therefore had to choose from among the top three candidates: Jackson, Adams, and William H. Crawford. Adams won after one ballot.

him politically, because the man was doing a good job administering the postal service.

Adams thought that the role of the national government was to do good for all the people. In his First Annual Message to Congress, he outlined an ambitious program that included building roads, canals, a national university, an astronomical observatory, and a naval academy similar to the U.S. Military Academy at West Point. The country needed a uniform standard of weights and measures, he said, and expeditions to explore more of the continent. Congress was horrified by this grand— and expensive—view of the federal government.

> "The great object of the institution of civil government is the improvement of the condition of those who are parties to the social compact, and no government, in whatever form constituted, can accomplish the lawful ends of its institution but in proportion as it improves the condition of those over whom it is established."
>
> — John Quincy Adams, First Annual Message to Congress, December 6, 1825

Adams's enemies had a good time making fun of him when he described observatories as "light-houses of the skies."

Congress began blocking his efforts right away. The new Latin American republics had invited the United States to a conference in Panama, but some congressmen didn't want to get involved with other countries. Southerners didn't like the fact that the Latin American countries had banned slavery. They were afraid that the conference might discuss extending the ban to North America. Congress finally approved two delegates to the convention, but because of the long delay, one arrived after the convention ended. The other died on the way. Congress also interfered with Adams's efforts to end a long-standing dispute on trading with Britain's colonies in the West Indies.

Adams bungled a conflict between the state of Georgia and the Creek tribe. In 1826, Georgia's governor tried to seize land belonging to the Creeks. Adams had never been sympathetic to the plight of the Native Americans, but this time he felt they were being treated unfairly. He sent a warning note to the governor, who sent back a defiant reply. Adams handed the problem over to Congress, which didn't want to interfere with the state's problems. The Creeks ended up with a treaty that cost them all their land.

In 1828, Congress passed a tariff that protected American manufactured goods by greatly increasing a tax on products made in foreign countries. Raw materials such as wool, hemp, and flax were also protected. The tariff favored the North and West at the expense of the South. Southerners called it the Tariff of Abominations. Adams didn't like this tariff, but he signed it anyway. In those days, presidents thought they should only veto or reject legislation if it violated the Constitution.

The tariff had two important results that had nothing to do with trade. First, it helped ensure that Adams would not be reelected. Second, it fueled the nullification movement in the South. In response to the tariff, Vice President John C. Calhoun, who was from South Carolina, wrote an essay saying that a state had a right to nullify or void any federal law that violated its rights. If three-fourths of the states then approved the law and it became part of the Constitution, the affected state had two choices. It could accept the law or secede from the Union. This issue of states' rights and nullification would become one of the central conflicts in American politics in the years leading to the Civil War (1861–1865).

LIFE IN THE WHITE HOUSE

Neither John Quincy nor Louisa enjoyed their time in the White House. She was attacked as a foreigner because she had been born in London to a British mother and American father. To this day, she remains the only First Lady born outside the United States.

The president found some solace in long walks and swimming in the Potomac. He regularly walked four miles, trying to improve his time each day. He also often went skinny-dipping in the Potomac River. In June 1825, he almost drowned. He and a servant took a canoe out on the river with the idea of swimming back to shore. The canoe started sinking, and Adams had to jump overboard half-clothed. "My principle difficulty," he wrote in his diary, "was in the loose sleeves of my shirt, which filled with water and hung like two fifty-six pound weights upon my arms."

Adams also spent time planting tree seeds and working in the garden at the White House. He kept silkworms, as well as an alligator given to him by the Marquis de Lafayette, the French hero of the American Revolution.

THE ELECTION OF 1828

The campaign for the next election began as soon as Adams took office. Seven months after Adams's inauguration, the Tennessee state legislature nominated Jackson for president. In 1828, Adams was the candidate of the

PRESIDENCY!!!

This is the House that We built.

TREASURY.

This is the malt that lay in the House that WE Built,

John Q. Adams,

This is the *MAIDEN* all forlorn, who worried herself from night till morn, to enter the House that We built.

CLAY,

This is the *MAN* all tattered and torn, who courted the maiden all forlorn, who worried herself from night till morn to enter the House that We built.

WEBSTER,

This is the *PRIEST*, all shaven and shorn, that married the man all tattered and torn, unto the maiden all forlorn, who worried herself from night till morn, to enter the House that We Built.

CONGRESS,

This is the BEAST, that carried the Priest all shaven and shorn, who married the man all tattered and torn, unto the maiden all forlorn, who worried herself from night till morn, to enter the House that We Built.

CABINET,

These are the *Rats* that pulled off their hats, and joined the Beast that carried the Priest all shaven and shorn, who married the man all tattered and torn unto the maiden all forlorn who worried herself from night till morn to enter the House that We built.

"OLD HICKORY,"

This is the *Wood*, well season'd and good, WE will use as a rod to whip out the RATS, that pulled off their hats and joined the Beast that carried the Priest all shaven and shorn, who married the man all tattered and torn, unto the maiden all forlorn, who worried herself from night till morn, to enter the House that We Built.

NEW-YORK.

This is the *state*, both early and late, that will strengthen the Wood well seasoned and good, to be used as a rod to whip out Rats that pulled off their hats, and joined the beast that carried the Priest all shaven and shorn, who married the man all tattered and torn unto the maiden all forlorn, who worried herself from night till morn to enter the House that WE Built.

EBONY & TOPAZ

* *The People.*

Andrew Jackson's campaign poster for the 1828 election criticized Adams and his followers. This campaign was the "dirtiest" U.S. presidential campaign to that date. Personal issues such as Louisa Adams's nationality and Rachel Jackson's divorce from her first husband became campaign fodder. Adams lost the election.

National Republican Party, and Jackson represented the Democratic Party. It was one of the nastiest campaigns in American history, with personal attacks on the candidates and their families. Jackson won both the popular vote and the electoral vote. In the electoral college, he received 178 votes to Adams's 83. To many voters, Adams represented the old-fashioned New England elite and a focus on the national government at the expense of the states. Jackson's win was proclaimed a victory for the common man, the western states, and the new Democratic Party.

For Jackson, the election brought personal sadness. In December 1828, his beloved wife, Rachel, died suddenly. Jackson blamed Adams's followers for her death. During the campaign, Jackson was accused of living with Rachel before she was divorced from her first husband. In reality, the Jacksons didn't know that Rachel's divorce was not final when they married.

Adams did not attend Jackson's inauguration, because the two men were bitter enemies. Only one other president had not attended his successor's inauguration: John Adams. The Adamses were also the only father and son to become presidents until George W. Bush, son of President George H.W. Bush, became president in 2000. Also, of the first seven presidents, they were the only two not elected to second terms. John Adams died in 1826, while his son was president. Now, in 1829, John Quincy Adams thought his own political life was over.

6

A Fighter in
the U.S. House

JOHN QUINCY ADAMS did not leave Washington when he moved out of the White House in 1829. Instead, he rented a house about two miles from the Capitol building. For the rest of his life, he would alternate between homes in Washington, D.C., and Quincy, Massachusetts. A part of him was glad that he was no longer president. He wrote in his diary, "No one knows, and few conceive, the agony of mind I have suffered from the time that I was made . . . a candidate for the Presidency till I was dismissed from that station by the failure of my re-election." He spent his days writing poetry, reading, and walking.

For the most part, though, in the months after leaving the

After leaving the presidency, Adams had to deal with personal problems such as the deaths of two sons and a brother. In the fall of 1830, Adams was elected to the U.S. House of Representatives. He was reelected eight times and began his fight against slavery. He also tried unsuccessfully to run for governor of Massachusetts.

White House, Adams was depressed. He was upset by more than the failure of his presidency. His oldest son, George, was having increasing trouble with alcohol and gambling. Adams decided that George should come to Washington, but on April 30, 1829, George disappeared overboard from a steamboat and drowned. He left behind large debts and a woman pregnant with his child. Unfortunately, that was not the end of the Adams family's problems with alcohol. Having already lost his brother Charles in 1800, Adams saw another brother, Thomas, die in 1832 and his second son, John, die in 1834, all from alcohol-related causes. At times, Adams admitted that he drank too much wine and vowed to cut down, but he never suffered the serious consequences of drinking that affected other members of his family.

ELECTION TO CONGRESS

In the fall of 1830, a Boston newspaper and a group of Adams's neighbors in Quincy suggested that he run for the U.S. House of Representatives. His family was appalled at the idea. Louisa said she wouldn't move to Washington if he won. His son, Charles Francis, thought it was a step down for a former president to take a seat in Congress. Adams was interested but told his neighbors that he wouldn't actively campaign. They also shouldn't expect him to favor any one political party or section of the country. In other words, he would remain as independent as ever. In November 1830, Adams was delighted to read in the newspaper that he had won. To this day, he is the only former president to later serve in the U.S. House. Louisa decided to go to Washington after all.

Adams's term of office did not start until the following year. When he took his seat in the House on December 5, 1831, he was 64 years old and about to start one of the most notable phases of his life. He was reelected to Congress eight times. He also tried to win one other office, running unsuccessfully for governor of Massachusetts in 1833.

> *"I have received nearly three votes in four throughout the district. My election as President of the United States was not half so gratifying to my inmost soul. No election or appointment conferred upon me ever gave me so much pleasure."*
> — John Quincy Adams, in his diary, November 7, 1830

THE GAG RULE

Adams hated slavery, calling it "the great and foul stain upon the North American Union." He didn't think much could be done to stop slavery in the states where it already existed, but he did oppose its spread to new states and territories. This was a common attitude at the time.

In the 1830s, abolitionists, who wanted to ban slavery everywhere, were sending petitions to Congress asking that slavery and the slave trade be stopped in Washington, D.C. Some abolitionists sent petitions to Adams. He didn't think that Congress had the legal authority to free slaves in the nation's capital and felt that abolition would lead to the breakup of the United States. Preserving the Union was extremely important to him: He had not approved when the New England states threatened to leave the Union during the War of 1812, and he did not want to see it destroyed now by abolition. Despite his moral objections

71

to slavery, he was an unlikely person to become an anti-slavery crusader.

Then the gag resolution or rule came up for a vote in Congress in 1836. The gag rule said that all petitions about slavery would be tabled, or laid aside, without being read or discussed. Adams believed that the Constitution guaranteed citizens the right to petition the government, and he was ready to fight hard—and loudly—for that. When his name was called to vote on the rule, Adams shouted, "I hold the resolution to be a direct violation of the Constitution of the United States, of the rules of this House, and of the rights of my constituents." The gag rule passed 117 to 68.

The gag rule expired at the end of each session of Congress, so it had to be voted on again every year. Adams kept trying to present petitions. He stood before the House and spoke for hours at a time. He got into shouting matches with other congressmen. Those who admired Adams called him "Old Man Eloquent." His enemies in the South called him "the Madman from Massachusetts."

Adams fought the gag rule for eight years. He felt that Southerners and Democrats had ruined his presidential administration; opposing slavery was one way to get back at them. Abolition was never going to be the answer for him, but he increasingly felt that something had to be done about the evils of slavery. As the years passed, Adams persuaded more congressmen to vote against the gag rule. In April 1844, a group of admirers gave him an ivory cane with the inscription "Right of Petition Triumphant." They asked him to add the date when the gag rule was finally defeated. That day came on December 3, 1844.

THE *AMISTAD* CASE

Adams's status within the antislavery movement also grew because of his role in the *Amistad* case. In 1839, a group of Africans was captured in West Africa and taken to Havana, Cuba. At the end of June, they were put on board the *Amistad*, a Spanish ship, which set sail for another Cuban port. One night, several Africans managed to break free. They killed the ship's captain and cook and took over the ship. They told the two remaining white men on board to sail toward Africa. By day the men did just that, but at night, they sailed north along the east coast of the United States. On August 26, 1839, an American naval ship seized the *Amistad* near Long Island, New York. The ship had 41 Africans on board: 37 men and four children. What would become of them now? That depended on whether they were considered slaves or free men.

Spain demanded the return of the ship, its cargo, and the Africans. If the Africans were slaves, then they were viewed as property and should be returned under the terms of several treaties signed by Spain and the United States. Both Spain and the United States had banned the international slave trade. This meant that slaves could not legally be brought into the United States or Cuba, which was a Spanish colony. Anyone brought into the United States as a slave was supposed to be sent back to Africa by the president. President Martin Van Buren, however,

---

ARGUMENT

OF

JOHN QUINCY ADAMS,

BEFORE THE

SUPREME COURT OF THE UNITED STATES,

IN THE CASE OF THE

UNITED STATES, APPELLANTS,

vs.

CINQUE, AND OTHERS, AFRICANS,

CAPTURED IN THE SCHOONER AMISTAD, BY LIEUT. GEDNEY,

DELIVERED ON THE 24th OF FEBRUARY AND 1st OF MARCH, 1841.

WITH A REVIEW OF THE CASE OF THE ANTELOPE,

REPORTED IN THE 10TH, 11TH AND 12TH VOLUMES OF WHEATON'S REPORTS.

———

NEW YORK:
S. W. BENEDICT, 128 FULTON STREET.
———
1841.

In 1839, a group of Africans on board the slave ship *Amistad* revolted, and the ship was seized by the American navy on August 26. Spain asked that the Africans be returned, but the case depended on whether the Africans were considered free or slaves. Adams argued the case before the Supreme Court on behalf of the Africans. The Africans won their freedom.

didn't want to get involved with the case as it slowly made its way through the American court system. He knew that if he freed the Africans, he would anger Southern voters, and 1840 was an election year.

Two lower courts ruled that the Africans were free, and then the case was appealed to the U.S. Supreme Court. Adams followed the case with interest. He offered his services as an adviser to the Africans' lawyers, but the lawyers wanted more. They wanted Adams to argue the case before the Supreme Court. At first, Adams said no. He was too busy in Congress, and at age 73, he thought he was too old. Besides, it had been at least 30 years since he had argued a case before the Supreme Court. Finally he agreed.

Arguments began on February 22, 1841. Adams addressed the court twice. Each time he took four hours, speaking forcefully for the captives' freedom. Adams argued that the Africans were not slaves and that according to the Declaration of Independence, they should be free. On March 9, Justice Joseph Story announced that the court had decided that the Africans were free.

> "The moment you come to the Declaration of Independence, that every man has a right to life and liberty, as an inalienable right, this case is decided. I ask nothing more on behalf of these unfortunate men, than this Declaration."
>
> — John Quincy Adams, *Amistad* argument before the Supreme Court, 1841

FINAL BATTLES AND TRIUMPHS

Adams enjoyed a good fight in Congress, especially if he could annoy the Southerners. In 1842, he presented a petition signed by some residents of Haverhill, Massachusetts, the town where he had studied Latin and Greek before attending Harvard. They called upon Congress to dissolve the Union because the federal government was spending too much money supporting the slave states. Southerners were outraged and called for Adams to be censured, or given an official reprimand. They hoped that this would lead to his leaving Congress. Adams defended himself, using his time before the House to attack the South and slavery. The measure to censure him was defeated in February 1842.

In 1836, while Adams was in Congress, the Republic of

PRESIDENT JOHN QUINCY ADAMS'S LEGACY

House of Representatives

John Quincy Adams thought that a good government should improve people's minds as well as their roads. In 1835, James Smithson, a British scientist, left an estate worth more than $500,000 to the United States for "an establishment for the increase and diffusion of knowledge." Adams, who was then serving in the House of Representatives, suggested setting up a House committee to handle the bequest, and, as a result, he was named chairman.

There were many ideas on how to spend the money, including a university, museum, library, and a scientific institute to conduct and publish research. Adams favored an astronomical observatory. Some congressmen, however, saw the Smithson bequest as a chance to get money for their own pet projects that had nothing to do with educating the public. For years, Adams fought off these congressmen and preserved the Smithson bequest for its original purpose. In 1846, Congress approved the formation of the Smithsonian Institution. Today the Smithsonian is the world's largest museum complex and welcomes about 30 million visitors annually to its museums in Washington, D.C. and New York City. It is also well known for its libraries and research centers, including one focusing on astronomy. The ivory cane that Adams received while fighting the gag rule is in its collection.

Texas declared its independence from Mexico. Some Americans wanted Texas to become part of the United States. Adams had always favored expanding the country's borders, but he was against the annexation of Texas. Many Americans were already living in Texas, and some of them owned slaves. Adams had always opposed the extension of slavery into new states. He feared that if Texas entered the Union, it would do so as a slave state or even states—Texas was so large that it could be divided into four or five states. Despite his opposition, Texas joined the Union on December 29, 1845.

Adams had also feared that admitting Texas to the Union could lead to war with Mexico, and he was right. The United States and Mexico disagreed over the border between Texas and Mexico. When Mexican soldiers crossed the Rio Grande River into Texas, the United States found a reason to declare war on May 13, 1846. Adams remained an opponent of the Mexican–American War for the rest of his life.

Because of his stand against slavery, Adams became more popular than he had ever been. In the summer of 1843, a family trip to New York state turned into a triumphant tour. Wherever he went, people came out to greet him. That same year, the Cincinnati Astronomical Society asked him to lay the cornerstone of a new observatory. It was a long and difficult journey from Massachusetts to Ohio. The weather was poor and Adams was sick, but he was happy to make the trip, glad to see that the United States would finally have one of his "light-houses of the sky."

On February 21, 1848, Adams suffered a second stroke while attending a House vote on whether to honor Mexican–American War soldiers. He died two days later in the office of the Speaker of the House at age 80.

In November 1846, Adams was walking in Boston when he collapsed. He appeared to have had a stroke. Everyone assumed that this was the end of his days as a congressman, but three months later, he returned to Congress. He served for another year. On February 21, 1848, Adams was at his desk in the House of Representatives. The House was voting on whether to honor some Mexican–American War soldiers. Always opposed to the war, Adams had just voted no when he suffered another stroke. Gravely ill, he was carried to the office of the Speaker of the House, where he died on February 23 at the age of 80.

From the time he was a child, Adams's whole life had been dedicated to serving the United States. He had always believed in serving the entire country, not just the interests of one state or one region, so it is fitting that John Quincy Adams, sixth president of the United States, died at the center of the national government, the U.S. Capitol building.

THE PRESIDENTS
OF THE
UNITED STATES

George Washington
1789–1797

John Adams
1797–1801

Thomas Jefferson
1801–1809

James Madison
1809–1817

James Monroe
1817–1825

John Quincy Adams
1825–1829

Andrew Jackson
1829–1837

Martin Van Buren
1837–1841

William Henry
Harrison
1841

John Tyler
1841–1845

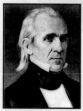
James Polk
1845–1849

Zachary Taylor
1849–1850

Millard Filmore
1850–1853

Franklin Pierce
1853–1857

James Buchanan
1857–1861

Abraham Lincoln
1861–1865

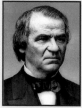
Andrew Johnson
1865–1869

Ulysses S. Grant
1869–1877

Rutherford B. Hayes
1877–1881

James Garfield
1881

Chester Arthur
1881–1885

Grover Cleveland
1885–1889

Benjamin Harrison
1889–1893

Grover Cleveland
1893-1897

William McKinley
1897–1901

Theodore Roosevelt
1901–1909

William H. Taft
1909–1913

Woodrow Wilson
1913–1921

Warren Harding
1921–1923

Calvin Coolidge
1923–1929

Herbert Hoover
1929–1933

Franklin D. Roo-
sevelt 1933–1945

Harry S. Truman
1945–1953

Dwight Eisenhower
1953–1961

John F. Kennedy
1961–1963

Lyndon Johnson
1963–1969

Richard Nixon
1969–1974

Gerald Ford
1974–1977

Jimmy Carter
1977–1981

Ronald Reagan
1981–1989

George H.W. Bush
1989–1993

William J. Clinton
1993–2001

George W. Bush
2001–

Note: Dates indicate years of
presidential service.
Source: www.whitehouse.gov

PRESIDENTIAL FACT FILE

THE CONSTITUTION

Article II of the Constitution of the United States outlines several requirements for the president of the United States, including:

- ★ **Age:** The president must be at least 35 years old.

- ★ **Citizenship:** The president must be a U.S. citizen.

- ★ **Residency:** The president must have lived in the United States for at least 14 years.

- ★ **Oath of Office:** On his inauguration, the president takes this oath: "I do solemnly swear (or affirm) that I will faithfully execute the office of President of the United States, and will to the best of my ability, preserve, protect and defend the Constitution of the United States."

- ★ **Term:** A presidential term lasts four years.

PRESIDENTIAL POWERS

The president has many distinct powers as outlined in and interpreted from the Constitution. The president:

- ★ Submits many proposals to Congress for regulatory, social, and economic reforms.

- ★ Appoints federal judges with the Senate's approval.

- ★ Prepares treaties with foreign nations to be approved by the Senate.

- ★ Can veto laws passed by Congress.

- ★ Acts as commander in chief of the military to oversee military strategy and actions.

- ★ Appoints members of the cabinet and many other agencies and administrations with the Senate's approval.

- ★ Can declare martial law (control of local governments within the country) in times of national crisis.

Presidential Fact File

TRADITION

Many parts of the presidency developed out of tradition. The traditions listed below are but a few that are associated with the U.S. presidency.

★ After taking his oath of office, George Washington added, "So help me God." Numerous presidents since Washington have also added this phrase to their oath.

★ Originally, the Constitution limited the term of the presidency to four years, but did not limit the number of terms a president could serve. Presidents, following the precedent set by George Washington, traditionally served only two terms. After Franklin Roosevelt was elected to four terms, however, Congress amended the Constitution to restrict presidents to only two.

★ James Monroe was the first president to have his inauguration outside the Capitol. From his inauguration in 1817 to Jimmy Carter's inauguration in 1977, it was held on the Capitol's east portico. Ronald Reagan broke from this tradition in 1981 when he was inaugurated on the west portico to face his home state, California. Since 1981, all presidential inaugurations have been held on the west portico of the Capitol.

★ Not all presidential traditions are serious, however. One of the more fun activities connected with the presidency began when President William Howard Taft ceremoniously threw out the first pitch of the new baseball season in 1910.  Presidents since Taft have carried on this tradition, including Woodrow Wilson, who is pictured here as he throws the first pitch of the 1916 season. In more recent years, the president has also opened the All-Star and World Series games.

Presidential Fact File

THE WHITE HOUSE

Although George Washington was involved with the planning of the White House, he never lived there. It has been, however, the official residence of every president beginning with John Adams, the second U.S. president. The

building was completed approximately in 1800, although it has undergone several renovations since then. It was the first public building constructed in Washington, D.C. The White House has 132 rooms, several of which are open to the public. Private rooms include those for administration and the president's personal residence. For an online tour of the White House and other interesting facts, visit the official White House website, *http://www.whitehouse.gov.*

THE PRESIDENTIAL SEAL

A committee began planning the presidential seal in 1777. It was completed in 1782. The seal appears as an official stamp on medals, stationery, and documents, among other items. Originally, the eagle faced right toward the arrows (a symbol of war) that it held in its talons. In 1945, President Truman had the seal altered so that the eagle's head instead faced left toward the olive branch (a symbol of peace), because he believed the president should be prepared for war but always look toward peace.

President Adams in Profile

PERSONAL

Name: John Quincy Adams

Birth date: July 11, 1767

Birth place: Braintree (now Quincy), Massachusetts

Father: John Adams

Mother: Abigail Smith

Wife: Louisa Johnson

Children: George, John, Charles, and Louisa

Death date: February 23, 1848

Death place: Washington, D.C.

POLITICAL

Years in office: 1825–1829

Vice president: John C. Calhoun

Occupations before presidency: Lawyer, diplomat, secretary of state

Political party: Democratic-Republican

Major achievements: Negotiated the Adams-Onis Treaty, which expanded the borders of the United States, and developed the Monroe Doctrine. As a congressman, he worked to repeal the Gag Rule on slavery.

Nickname: Old Man Eloquent

Tribute:

Adams National Historic Park
(Quincy, MA; *http://www.nps.gov/adam/*), which includes John Quincy Adams's birthplace and the United First Parish Church, where Adams is buried with his wife and parents.

CHRONOLOGY

1767 John Quincy Adams is born on July 11 in Braintree (now Quincy), Massachusetts.

1778 John Adams takes Johnny with him to France for the first time.

1779 Johnny sails for France again and begins his diary.

1781 Johnny travels to Russia to serve as Francis Dana's secretary and translator.

1787 John Quincy Adams graduates from Harvard College and begins studying law.

1790 At his parents' request, he begins practicing law in Boston.

1791 The Publicola letters are published.

1794 George Washington appoints him minister to the Netherlands.

1797 Adams marries Louisa Catherine Johnson, and his father appoints him minister to Prussia.

1802 Adams is elected to the Massachusetts State Senate.

1803 Adams is elected to the U.S. Senate.

1809 James Madison appoints him minister to Russia.

1814 Adams negotiates Treaty of Ghent, ending the War of 1812.

1815 James Madison appoints him minister to Great Britain.

1817 President James Monroe names him secretary of state.

1819 Adams negotiates Adams–Onis Treaty, extending U.S. border to the Pacific.

1823 Adams encourages President Monroe to support the policy that will become the Monroe Doctrine.

1825 Adams is inaugurated as the sixth president of the United States.

1830 Adams is elected to U.S. House of Representatives for term beginning in 1831.

1841 Adams argues the *Amistad* case before the U.S. Supreme Court.

1844 The gag resolution is defeated.

1848 Adams dies at U.S. Capitol on February 23.

Bober, Natalie S. *Abigail Adams: Witness to a Revolution.* New York: Aladdin Paperbacks, 1998.

———. *Countdown to Independence: A Revolution of Ideas in England and Her American Colonies: 1760–1776.* New York: Atheneum Books for Young Readers, 2001.

Brookhiser, Richard. *America's First Dynasty: The Adamses, 1735–1918.* New York: The Free Press, 2002.

Current, Richard N., T. Harry Williams, and Frank Freidel. *The Essentials of American History.* New York: Alfred A. Knopf, 1972.

Dupuy, R. Ernest and Trevor R. Dupuy. *The Encyclopedia of Military History from 3500 B.C. to the Present.* New York: Harper & Row Publishers, 1977.

Elliot, Ian, ed. *James Monroe: 1758–1831 Chronology, Documents, Bibliographical Aids.* Dobbs Ferry, N.Y.: Oceana Publications, Inc., 1969.

Greenblatt, Miriam. *John Quincy Adams: Sixth President of the United States.* Presidents of the United States series. Ada, Okla.: Garrett Educational Corporation, 1990.

Hewson, Martha S. *The Electoral College.* YOUR GOVERNMENT: HOW IT WORKS series. Philadelphia: Chelsea House Publishers, 2002.

Jones, Kenneth, ed. *John Quincy Adams: 1767–1848 Chronology, Documents, Bibliographical Aids.* Dobbs Ferry, N.Y.: Oceana Publications, Inc., 1970.

Koch, Adrienne and William Peden, eds. *The Selected Writings of John and John Quincy Adams.* New York: Alfred A. Knopf, 1946.

McCullough, David. *John Adams.* New York: Simon & Schuster, 2002.

Myers, Walter Dean. *Amistad: A Long Road to Freedom.* New York: Dutton, 1998.

Nagel, Paul C. *John Quincy Adams: A Public Life, A Private Life.* Cambridge, Mass.: Harvard University Press, 1999.

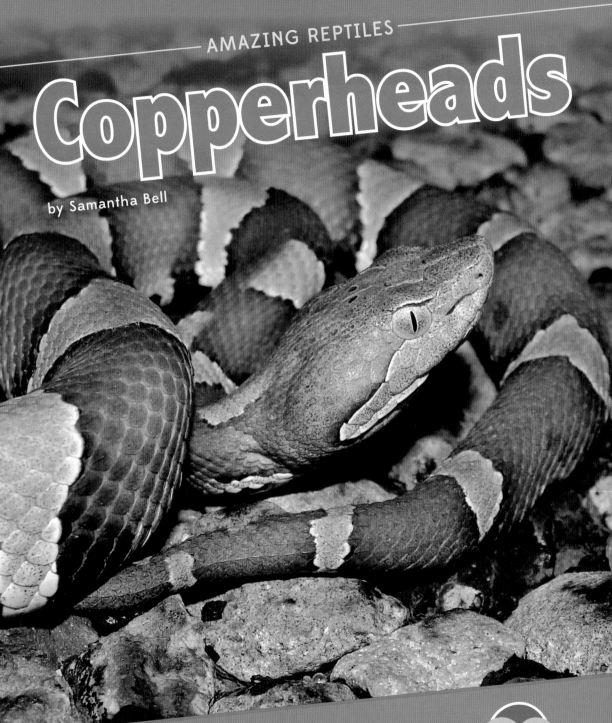

AMAZING REPTILES

Copperheads

by Samantha Bell

Content Consultant
Leonard Jones, BA
Graduate Student, Leache Lab
University of Washington

Core Library

An Imprint of Abdo Publishing
www.abdopublishing.com

www.abdopublishing.com

Published by Abdo Publishing, a division of ABDO, PO Box 398166,
Minneapolis, Minnesota 55439. Copyright © 2015 by Abdo Consulting
Group, Inc. International copyrights reserved in all countries. No part of
this book may be reproduced in any form without written permission from
the publisher. Core Library™ is a trademark and logo of Abdo Publishing.

Printed in the United States of America, North Mankato, Minnesota
032014
092014

THIS BOOK CONTAINS
RECYCLED MATERIALS

Cover Photo: Matt Jeppson/Shutterstock Images
Interior Photos: Matt Jeppson/Shutterstock Images, 1, 8 (top), 16;
iStockphoto, 4, 7; Shutterstock Images, 8 (middle top), 8 (bottom), 34; Eric
Isselee/Shutterstock Images, 8 (middle bottom); iStockphoto/Thinkstock,
11, 18, 28, 43; Robert Hamilton/Alamy, 12; Joe McDonald/Corbis, 15;
Animals Animals/SuperStock, 20, 36, 38; Paul Wood/Alamy, 23; Design
Pics/Thinkstock, 25, 45; Red Line Editorial, 30; George Grall/National
Geographic Creative, 33; Derrick Hamrick/Glow Images, 40

Editor: Mirella Miller
Series Designer: Becky Daum

Library of Congress Control Number: 2014932339

Cataloging-in-Publication Data
Bell, Samantha.
 Copperheads / Samantha Bell.
  p. cm. -- (Amazing reptiles)
Includes bibliographical references and index.
ISBN 978-1-62403-371-1
1. Copperhead--Juvenile literature.   I. Title.
597.96/3--dc23

2014932339

CONTENTS

CHAPTER ONE

Seeking Out Prey

A deer mouse scurries out of hiding as the moon slips behind a cloud. But the darkness of the forest isn't enough to protect the mouse. Coiled up on fallen leaves and laying completely still, a copperhead snake waits. It senses the mouse is nearby. The copperhead remains motionless. It is in no hurry. It has been waiting for hours. The mouse moves within striking distance, and the copperhead senses

Copperheads belong to the pit viper snake group. Pit vipers are easy to recognize by their triangle-shaped heads.

its chance. With one quick strike of its fangs, the copperhead has found its next meal.

Like other snakes, copperheads are classified as reptiles. They have a backbone, breathe with lungs, and are cold-blooded. Copperheads also have scaly skin. These scales prevent them from drying out. They also protect the snake as it moves over rough ground.

Built to Hide

Copperheads belong to one of the largest groups of poisonous snakes, the pit vipers. This group also includes rattlesnakes and cottonmouths. Pit vipers have pits located on

Let's Not Meet

Many of the poisonous snakebites reported in the United States each year come from copperheads. These snakes are not aggressive, however. They would rather avoid humans. But when they feel threatened, they stay completely still. Because they blend in so well with their surroundings, people often do not see them until it is too late. If someone steps on or near a copperhead, it bites to protect itself. They often give a warning bite. While these bites can be painful and cause severe illness, they rarely lead to death.

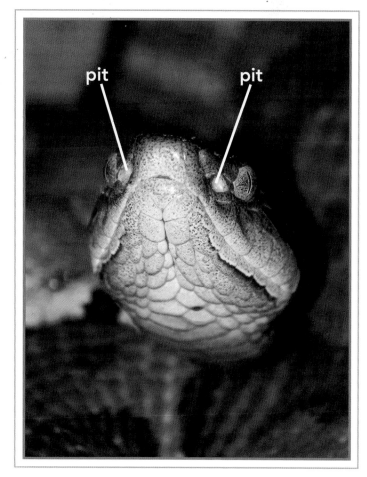

pit pit

Snakes use these pits to detect their preys' body heat.

the sides of their faces between their eyes and their nostrils. These pits help the snakes detect heat. Even in the dark, pit vipers can accurately strike their prey.

All five subspecies of copperheads are found only in North America. These include the northern, the southern, the Trans-Pecos, the Osage, and the broad-banded copperheads. Most copperheads grow

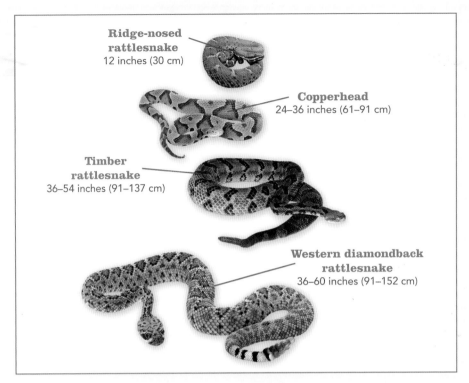

Ridge-nosed rattlesnake
12 inches (30 cm)

Copperhead
24–36 inches (61–91 cm)

Timber rattlesnake
36–54 inches (91–137 cm)

Western diamondback rattlesnake
36–60 inches (91–152 cm)

Medium-Sized Snakes

After reading about how big copperheads grow, did you imagine them to be big snakes? This chart shows the average size of a copperhead compared with other pit vipers found in the United States. How does looking at this chart change your ideas about the size of copperheads? Does seeing this chart help you understand why scientists call copperheads medium-sized snakes?

to be approximately 24 to 36 inches (61 to 91 cm) long. Copperheads usually weigh less than 1 pound (0.5 kg). The longest copperhead on record was more than 48 inches (122 cm) long.

BIBLIOGRAPHY

Nevins, Allan, ed. *The Diary of John Quincy Adams 1794–1845: American Diplomacy, and Political, Social, and Intellectual Life, from Washington to Polk.* New York: Charles Scribner's Sons, 1951.

Peterson, Merrill D. *The Great Triumverate: Webster, Clay and Calhoun.* New York: Oxford University Press, 1987.

Remini, Robert V. *John Quincy Adams.* New York: Times Books, Henry Holt and Co., 2002.

————. *The Life of Andrew Jackson.* New York: Penguin Books, 1988.

Russell, Francis. *Adams: An American Dynasty.* New York: American Heritage Press, 1976.

Shields-West, Eileen. *The World Almanac of Presidential Campaigns.* New York: World Almanac, 1992.

Taylor, Robert J., ed. *Diary of John Quincy Adams.* Vols. I–II. Cambridge, Mass.: Belknap Press of Harvard University Press, 1981.

FURTHER READING

Bober, Natalie S. *Abigail Adams: Witness to a Revolution.* New York: Aladdin Paperbacks, 1998.

Hewson, Martha S. *The Electoral College.* YOUR GOVERNMENT: HOW IT WORKS series. Philadelphia: Chelsea House Publishers, 2002.

Myers, Walter Dean. *Amistad: A Long Road to Freedom.* New York: Dutton, 1998.

Remini, Robert V. *John Quincy Adams.* New York: Times Books, Henry Holt and Co., 2002.

Shields-West, Eileen. *The World Almanac of Presidential Campaigns.* New York: World Almanac, 1992.

WEBSITES

Miller Center of Public Affairs: The American President.
http://www.americanpresident.org

Smithsonian Institution. History.
http://www.si.edu/about/history.htm

Smithsonian Institution: Ivory Cane Given to John Quincy Adams in 1844.
http://www.smithsonianlegacies.si.edu/objectdescription.cfm?ID=60

The White House. All Creatures Great and Small.
http://www.whitehouse.gov/holiday/2002/petsculptures/04.html

INDEX

Picture Credits

ACKNOWLEDGMENTS

Thank you to Celebrity Speakers Intl. for coordinating Mr. Cronkite's contribution to this book.

Martha S. Hewson is a freelance writer and editor who works on projects for children and adults. Like John Quincy Adams, she earned a bachelor of arts degree from Harvard University. She also has a master's degree in journalism from Columbia University. A former editor at *The Philadelphia Inquirer* and *McCall's* magazine, she is the author of two other Chelsea House books: *Stonewall Jackson* in the FAMOUS FIGURES OF THE CIVIL WAR series and *The Electoral College* in the YOUR GOVERNMENT: HOW IT WORKS series. She lives with her family near Philadelphia.

Walter Cronkite has covered virtually every major news event during his more than 60 years in journalism, during which he earned a reputation for being "the most trusted man in America." He began his career as a reporter for the United Press during World War II, taking part in the beachhead assaults of Normandy and covering the Nuremberg trials. He then joined *CBS News* in Washington, D.C., where he was the news anchor for political convention and election coverage from 1952 to 1980. CBS debuted its first half-hour weeknight news program with Mr. Cronkite's interview of President John F. Kennedy in 1963. Mr. Cronkite was inducted into the Academy of Television Arts and Sciences in 1985 and has written several books. He lives in New York City with his wife of 59 years.